with Cleve Taylor

Text written with and photography by
Jeffrey B. Snyder

Illustrations by Bruce Day

Schiffer Publishing Ltd

4880 Lower Valley Road, Atglen, PA 19310

To my motorcycle Mama, Sandy. I appreciate your understanding and support during my life crises.

Copyright © 1999 by Cleve Taylor
Library of Congress catalog Card Number: 98-87281

Designed by Laurie A. Smucker
Typeset in Swiss 721BT

ISBN: 0-7643-0647-2
Printed in China

Contents

Published by Schiffer Publishing Ltd.
4880 Lower Valley Road
Atglen, PA 19310
Phone: (610) 593-1777; Fax: (610) 593-2002
E-mail: Schifferbk@aol.com
Please write for a free catalog.
This book may be purchased from the publisher.
Please include $3.95 for shipping.

In Europe, Schiffer books are distributed by
Bushwood Books
6 Marksbury Avenue
Kew Gardens
Surrey TW9 4JF England
Phone: 44 (0) 181 392-8585; Fax: 44 (0) 181 392-9876
E-mail: Bushwd@aol.com
Please try your bookstore first.

We are interested in hearing from authors
with book ideas on related subjects.

Introduction

I wish that I could entertain you with wonderful stories of characters that I encountered during my motorcycle riding days, but I can't. The truth is that I was too frightened to interact with the more interesting ones and too uninterested in the less interesting riders. Thus, I have no stories.

I wish that I could tell you that the motorcycles characters I carve are caricatures of real life bikers, but I can't. The truth is that the bikers I saw in bars and other popular gathering places would have made great caricatures but I didn't want them to catch me staring for periods of time long enough to store their images in my mental scrapebook. And the bikers I passed on the road were generally go-ing too fast for me to capture details of their expressions. Thus, I have no real likenesses on which to carve caricatures.

The bike and rider that are photographed as I carved them in this book were taken from a painting done by a good friend, Bruce Day. He is a great artist, specializing in caricature art. As a free lancer, he is much in demand among advertising agencies, magazines, and collectors of humorous art. Bruce's studio is located at 6080 Arney Lane, Boise, Idaho 83703.

Thanks Bruce for both the wonderful ideas and your art work.

Tools

Here are the tools you will need for this project: I recommend a Kevlar carving glove impervious to knife cuts, a series of bench knives, a Foredom or Dremel rotary power tool with a Kutzall burr, and a band saw. The gouges I use include a 1/4" #9 gouge, 1/2" #3 fishtail gouge, three different size V tools (1/4", 1/8", and a micro 2mm or 1/16" V gouge), a 3/16" deep gouge, a 1/8" #5, and a 1/2" #7 gouge, and a 3/32" deep gouge (deep gouges are also called veiners).

Carving the Motorcyclist and his Bike

Pattern Specs

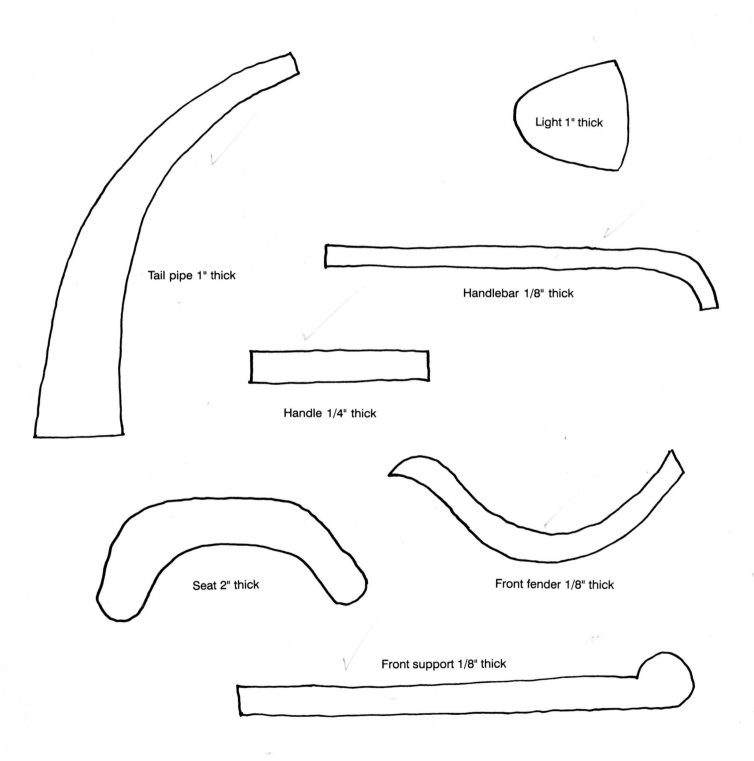

Light 1" thick

Tail pipe 1" thick

Handlebar 1/8" thick

Handle 1/4" thick

Seat 2" thick

Front fender 1/8" thick

Front support 1/8" thick

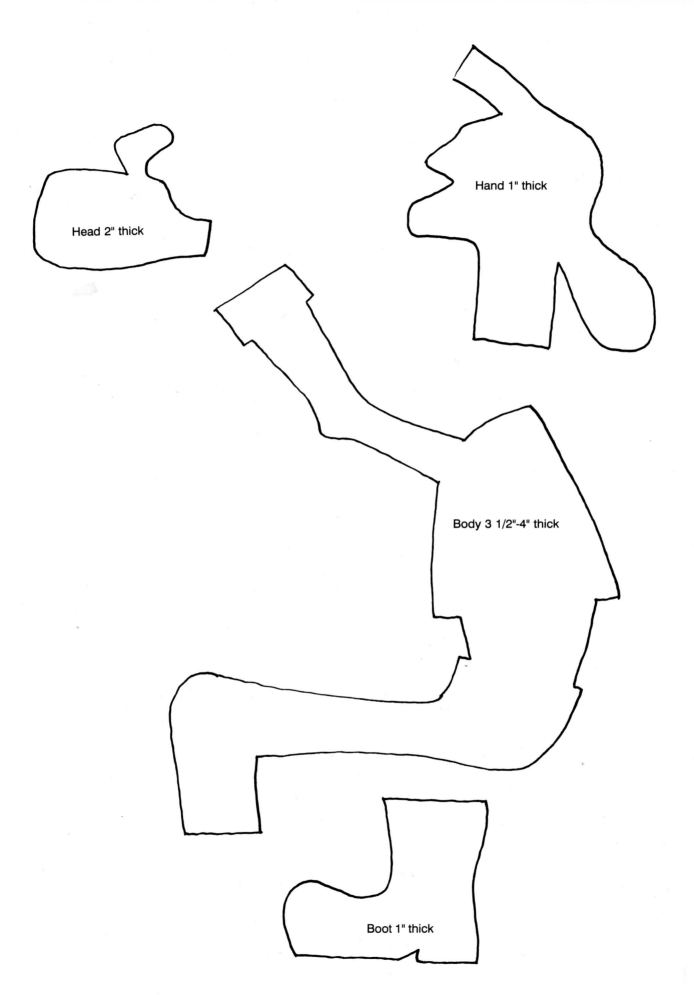

Head 2" thick

Hand 1" thick

Body 3 1/2"-4" thick

Boot 1" thick

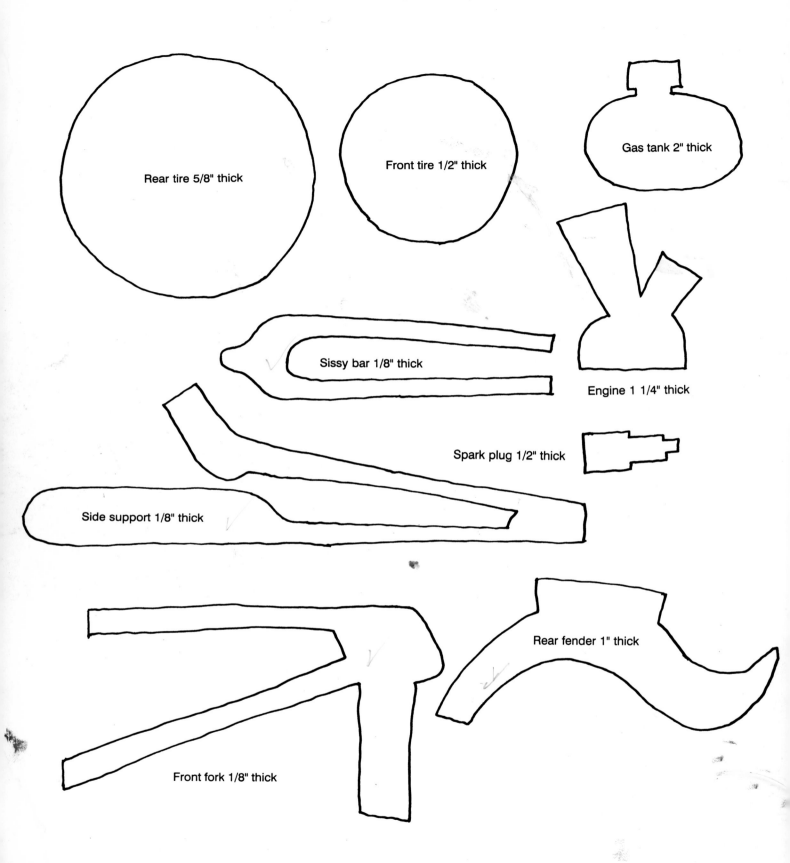

Rear tire 5/8" thick

Front tire 1/2" thick

Gas tank 2" thick

Sissy bar 1/8" thick

Engine 1 1/4" thick

Spark plug 1/2" thick

Side support 1/8" thick

Rear fender 1" thick

Front fork 1/8" thick

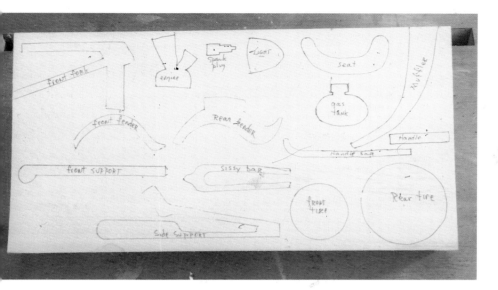

Transfer the motorcycle patterns onto a 2" thick x 14" long basswood blank. Use a bandsaw to cut these pieces out. The thickness for each piece is shown on the plan drawing.

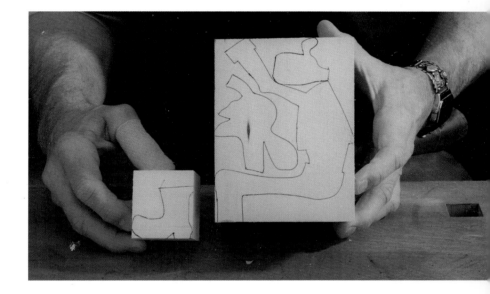

Laying out the body, head, hand and boots for the motorcycle rider. The body, head, and hand patterns are transferred to a 3.5" thick x 4.5" wide x 6" tall block of basswood. The boots are laid out on a 2" x 2" x 2" block.

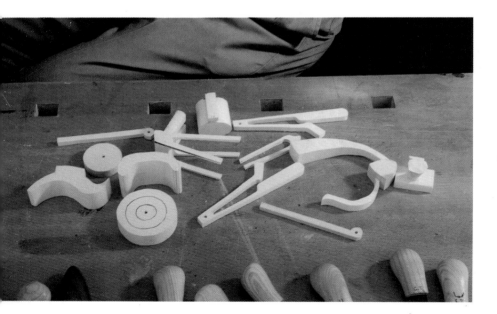

The pieces of the motorcycle have been cut

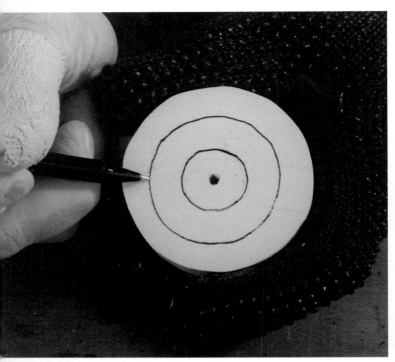

Use a compass to draw the wheel and tire for the rear of the bike. The front wheel of the bike will be drawn in a similar manner.

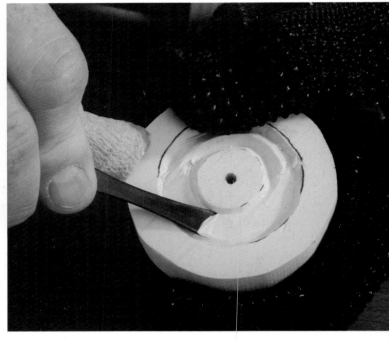

Relieve between the two V cuts to a depth of about 1/8".

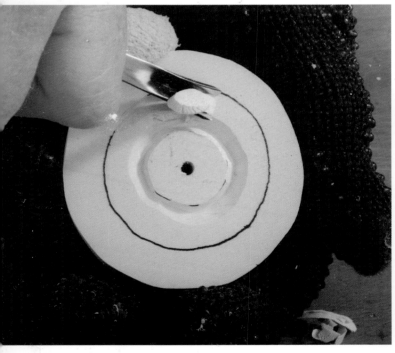

Use a large V tool to outline the wheel.

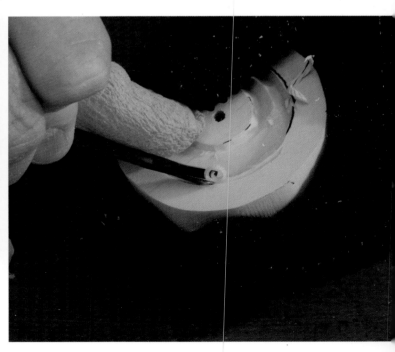

Cut in the rim of the wheel.

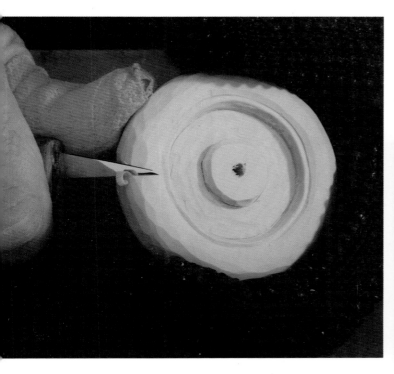

After cutting in the wheel on both sides, round the tire from rim to rim.

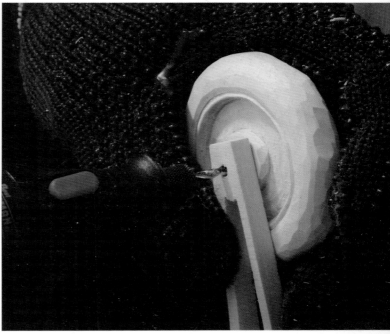

Drill a 1/8" diameter hole through the side support and through the rear wheel to contain the rear axle.

Front and rear tires completed.

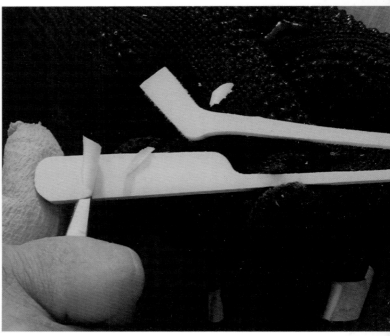

Using a bench knife, and/or flat gouges, clean saw marks from both side supports.

The side support and rear wheel centered. Use a 1/8"
diameter dowel as an axle, passing it through both side
supports and the wheel. Trim the ends of the dowel flush to
the side supports. You may choose to glue the dowel;
however, it is not necessary to do so.

Setting the rear aside for now, round the front forks and carve
a 1/8" diameter nipple on the end of each fork.

These protrusions at the front of the front fork assembly are
springs. Use a large V tool and cut the spring coils in skewed
to the centerline.

The front fork is carved. Drill a 1/8" diameter hole through the side to receive the handlebars.

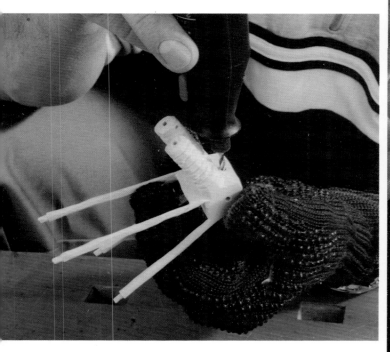

Drill 1/8" diameter holes in the end of each spring and along the centerline as indicated.

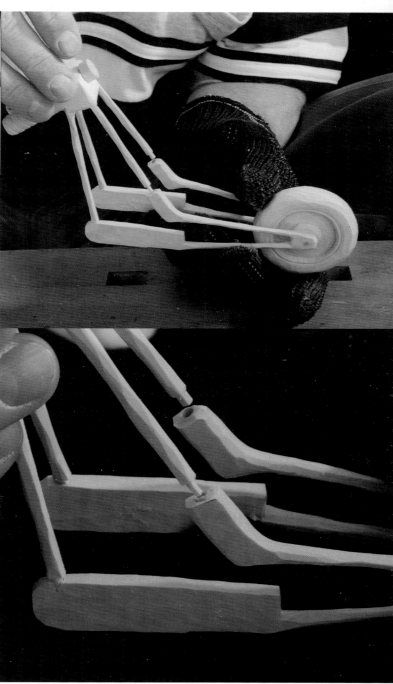

Insert the nipples carved on the front struts into the 1/8" diameter holes drilled into the side supports.

After rounding the front support, carving a 1/8" diameter nipple on the upper ends, and drilling a 1/8" diameter hole through each support and into the wheel, assemble the front end with a 1/8" diameter dowel.

Round the top side of the motorcycle seat.

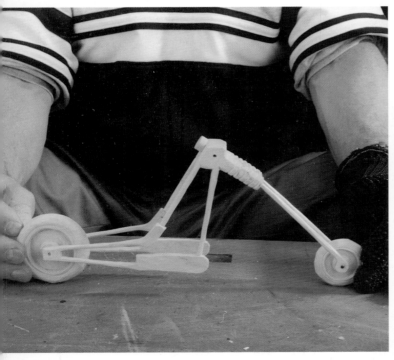

The bike assembly to this point.

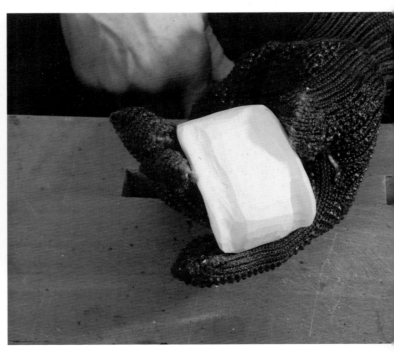

The underside of the bike seat is grooved using a 1/4" wide deep gouge to fit over the side supports.

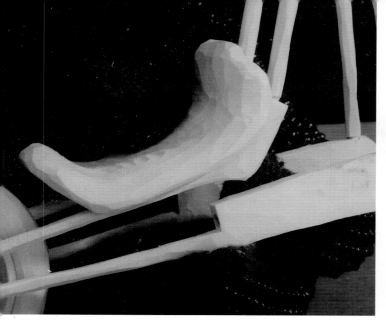

Like so.

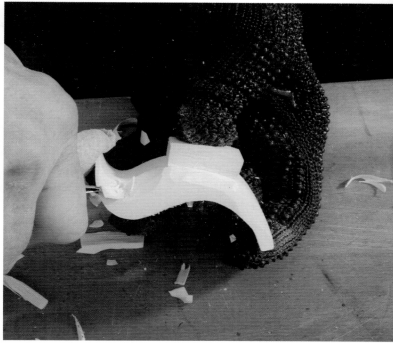

Using your knife and gouges, round off the top of the rear fender.

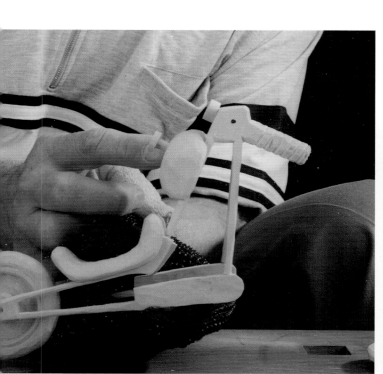

In a similar fashion round the top and groove the underside of the gas can, fitting the can to the front forks.

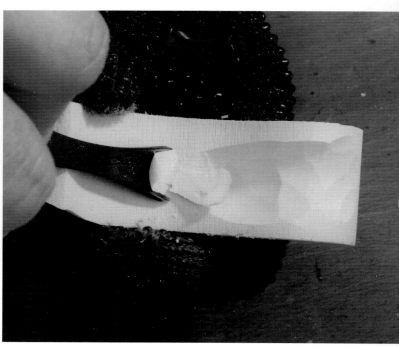

Using a wide gouge, groove the underside of the rear fender, like so.

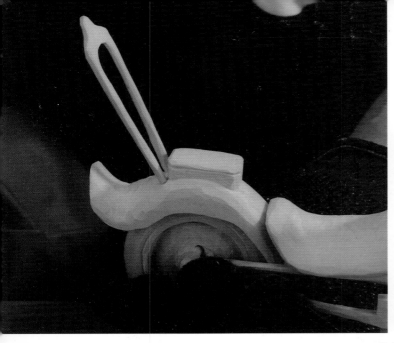

The rear fender with the rounded sissy bar attached.

After rounding the outside of the motor, use a V tool to carve simulated cooling fins around the cylinder.

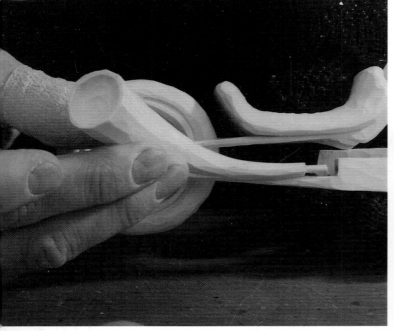

The muffler has been rounded and a 1/8" diameter nipple has been carved at the small end to fit into the hole drilled into the side support.

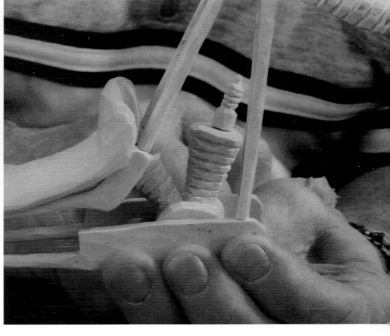

The carved engine, complete with an inserted spark plug, is shown between the side supports.

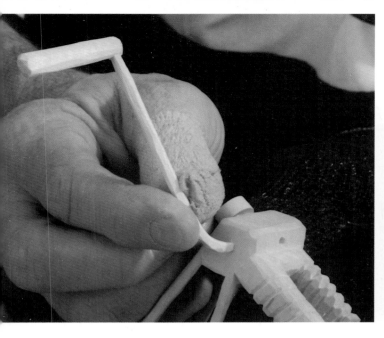

Using a knife, carve, round, and then assemble the handlebars. The completed handlebar assembly.

The front fender is shown between the front forks.

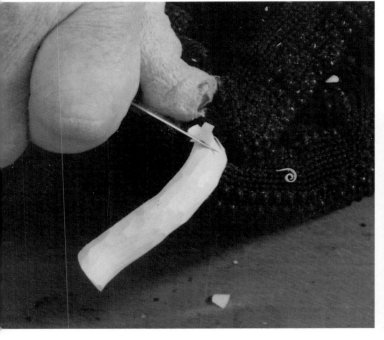

Round off the front fender.

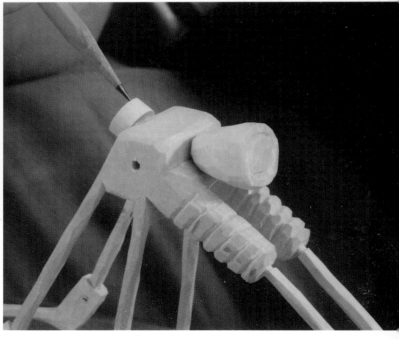

The carved headlight is held in place with glued doweling. A short piece of 1/2" dowel, glued in place, serves as a speedometer. The pencil points to the speedometer.

Begin carving the rider by cleaning up and rounding of the motorcycle rider's body using a bench knife and gouges.

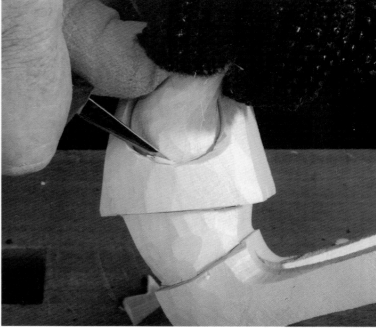

After relieving the arm to the bottom of the vest's V cut, undercut the vest so that the arm appears to extend out from beneath it.

After rounding the arm and side, use a large V tool to cut an arm hole in the vest.

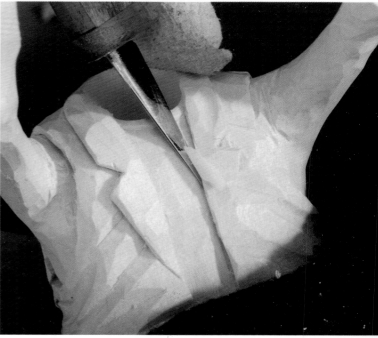

In a similar manner, cut in the front of the vest and undercut the vest to indicate the chest underlying the vest.

Use a small V tool to cut in a necklace around the neck hole.

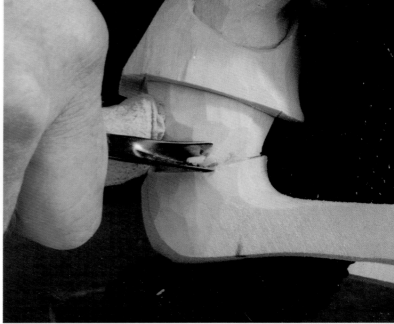

Use a V tool to cut in the bottom of the vest and the top of the pant line around the body.

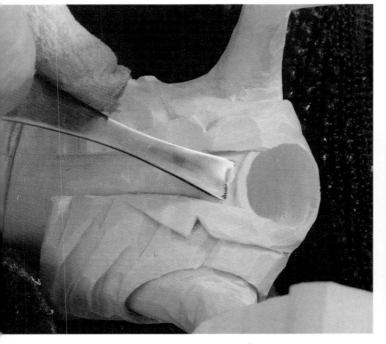

Relieve the chest to the bottom of necklace cut. There are two reasons for this necklace: the first is that it looks good and most motorcyclists wear them; the second reason is that we are inserting the head into the neck and we need to hide the insertion line.

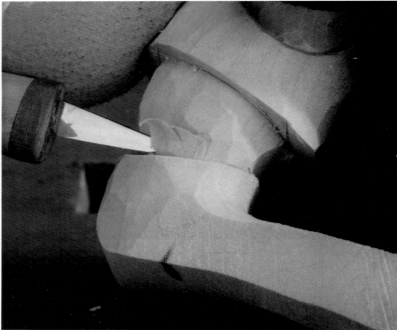

Use your knife to relieve the body between the bottom of the vest and the top of the pant line.

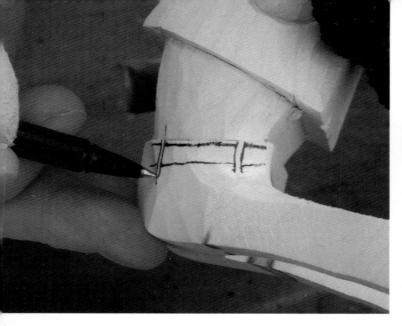

Sketch in belt loops and the belt.

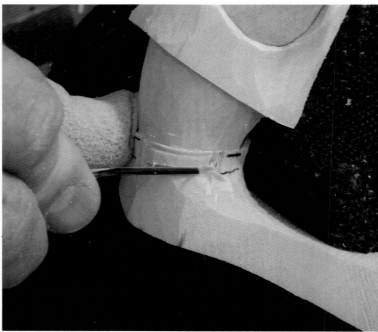

Cut in the top and bottom of the belt.

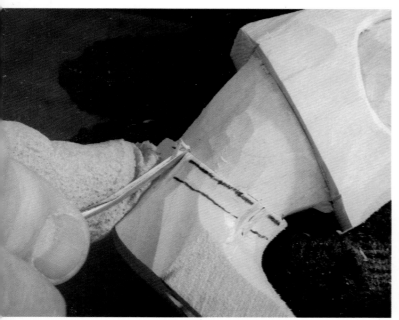

Using a small V tool, cut in the belt loops.

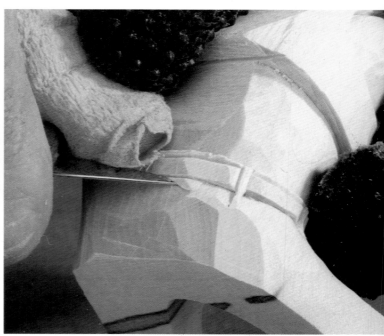

Relieve the pants, both above and below the belt.

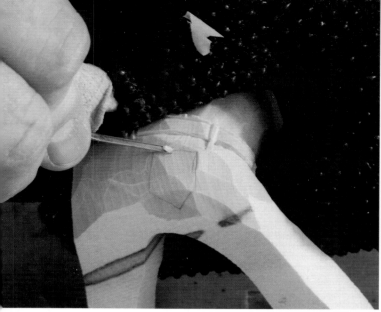

Rear pockets can be outlined with the small V tool.

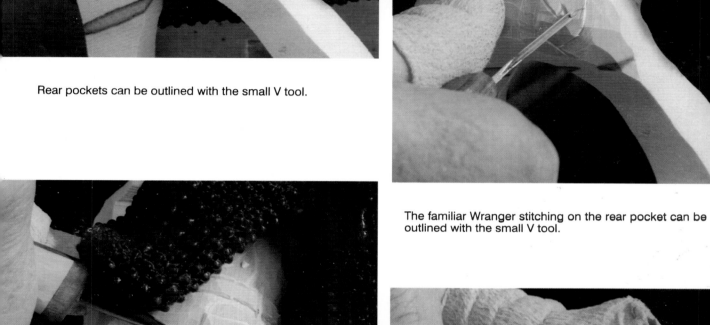

The familiar Wranger stitching on the rear pocket can be outlined with the small V tool.

Use your knife to relieve excess wood away from around the pocket. Knife-relieved pocket.

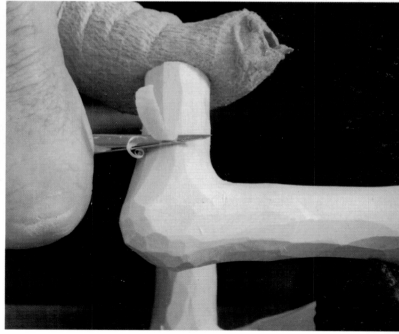

Continue to round off the legs.

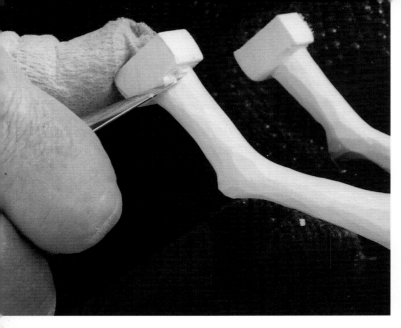

Round off the arms up to the bracelets.

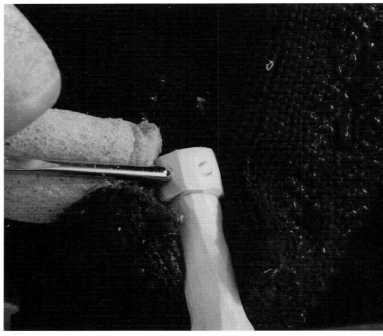

Using a 1/8" half round gouge, cut in a series of studs around the circumference of the bracelet. It is important to insert the gouge at an angle of about 45 degrees to the vertical center line of the stud in order to reduce the chances of the stud popping out.

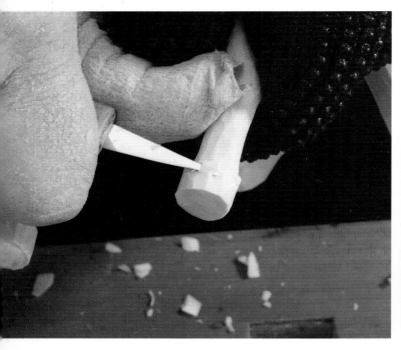

Round off the leather bracelets.

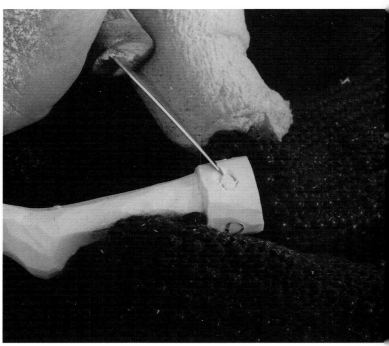

Use a knife to relieve around these studs.

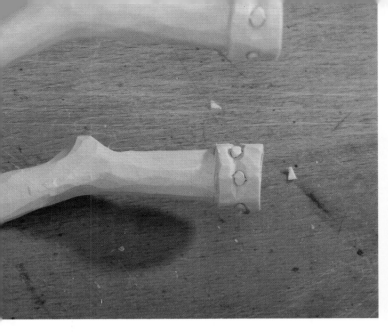

The wood has been relieved around the studs.

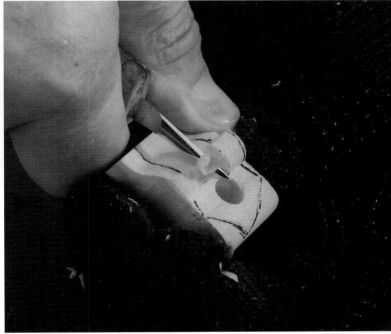

Cut in the thumb using your knife.

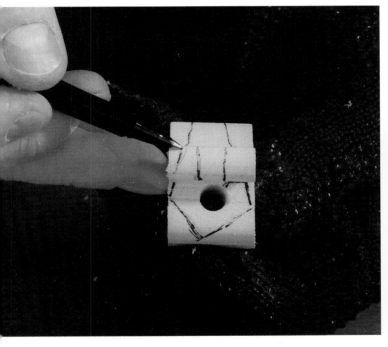

Sketch in the location of the thumb and other prominent features of the hand (including the wrist and fingers) on the blank for the right hand as shown. Drill a 5/16" diameter hole through the hand, as shown, to receive the handle of the motorcycle handlebar.

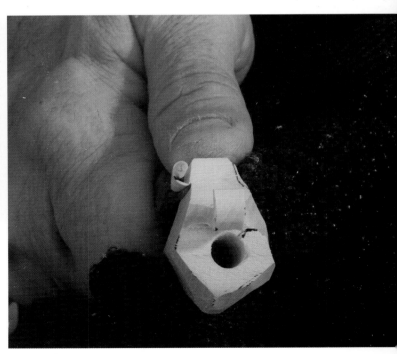

Cut in the wrist and the other fingers as well.

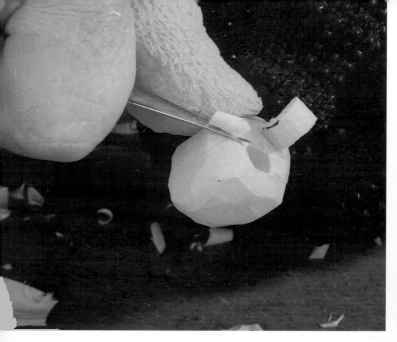

Round off the fingers and the wrist.

Cut in the ends of the finger using your knife.

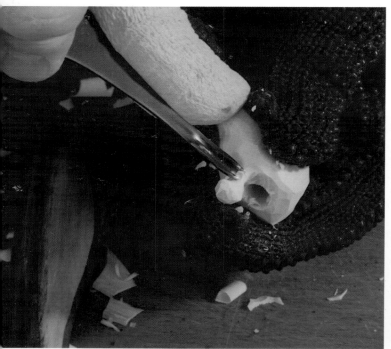

Using your knife and a small deep gouge, round off the thumb.

Cut in the separation between the fingers with a large V tool.

Use your knife to round off the fingers.

Use a small V tool to cut in the finger nails.

Use your knife tip to widen and deepen the separation between the fingers.

You can also use your small V tool to cut in some of the wrinkles around the knuckles.

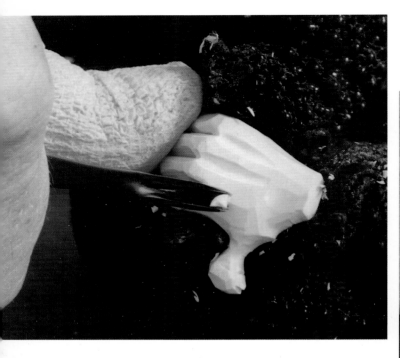

Use a small deep gouge to make cuts suggestive of the ligaments between the fingers.

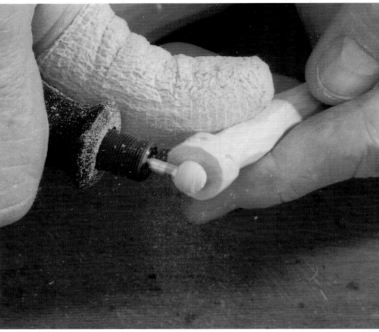

Use a small Kutzall Burr and create a socket at the end of each wrist into which a hand will fit.

Round off the wrist like a ball.

The ball that you carved on the end of the hand and the socket in the end of the arm should allow the hand to sit in the arm like this.

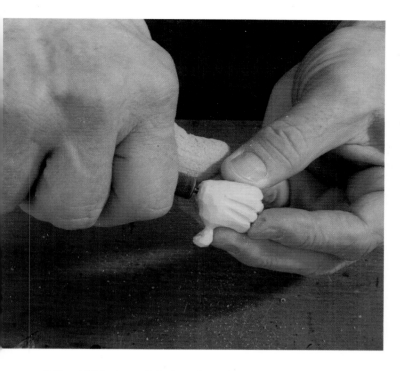

Drill a 1/8" hole straight into the wrist.

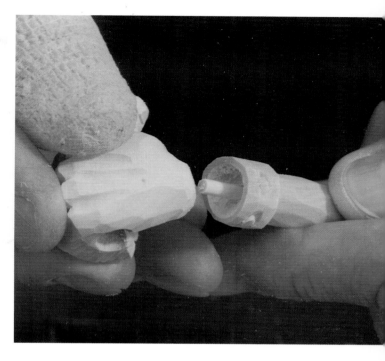

Insert a 1/8" dowel into the arm hole and insert the hand over the dowel, connecting the hand to the arm.

Drill a 1/8" hole straight into the arm.

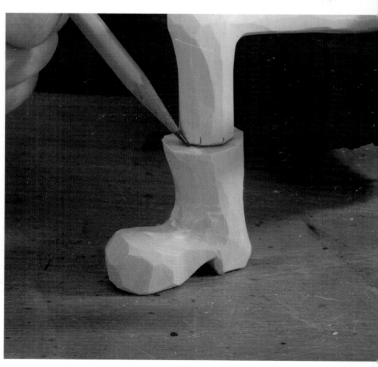

After rounding the boot, trace around the base of the leg to provide a guide line for inserting the leg into the boot.

With a large V tool, cut this opening into the top of the boot, following the pencil guide line.

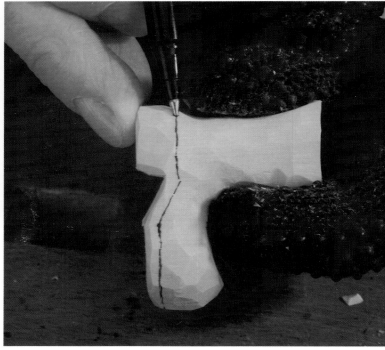

Draw in the heel and sole of the boot.

Relieve the top of the boot to a depth of about 1/8".

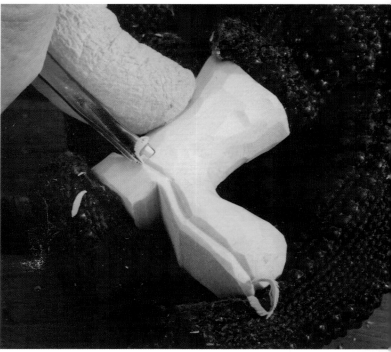

Cut along this line with a large V tool.

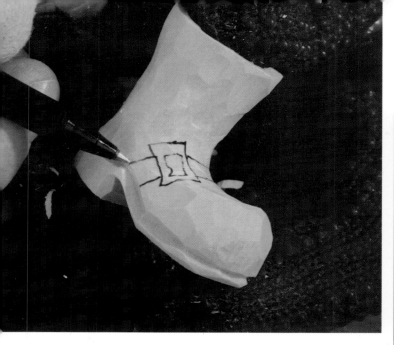

Sketch in a large buckle and strap across the boot.

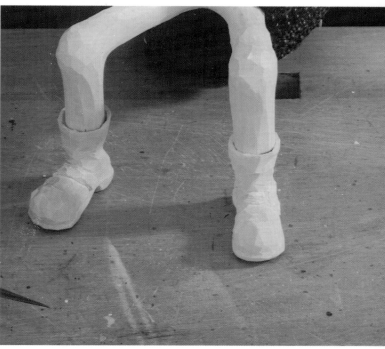

This is what the boots look like so far.

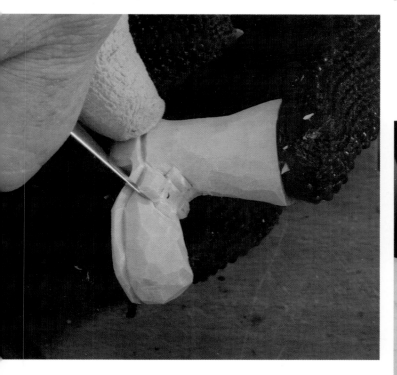

Relieve the boot to heighten the presence of the buckle and strap.

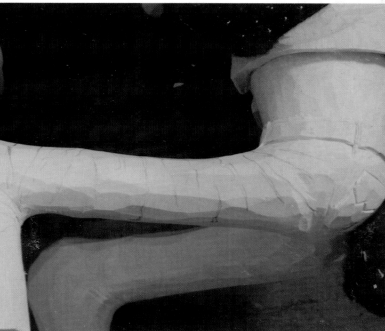

The wrinkles on the pant leg will follow a pattern similar to this.

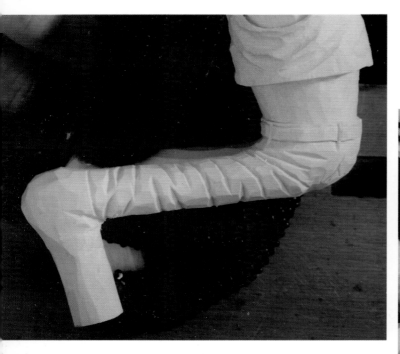

Use a large V tool to cut these wrinkles in initially.

Wrinkles completed.

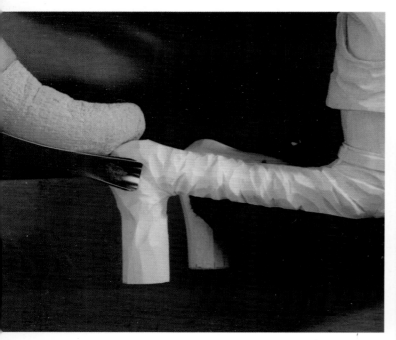

Using large and small gouges alternately, we can open up some of these V cuts, smooth over others, and totally obliterate some more. Keep doing this until you like what you have or until you have completely carved away the wood from the leg. If the latter occurs, you might think about starting over with a new blank or, I suppose, you could have a short-legged rider.

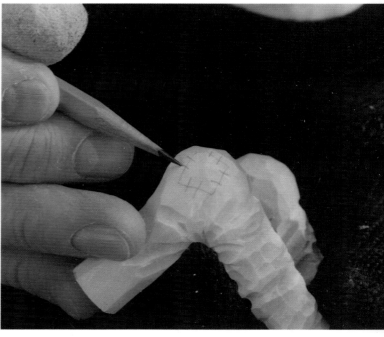

This knee is a great area for a patch.

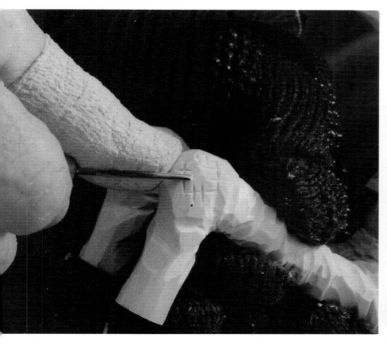

Use a small V tool the cut that patch in.

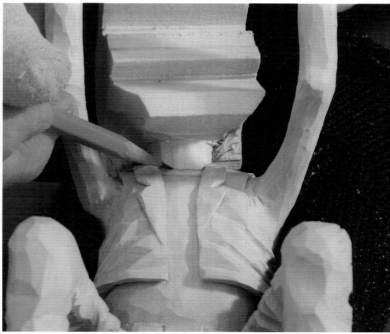

I am drawing a reference line around the neck along the top of the neck hole.

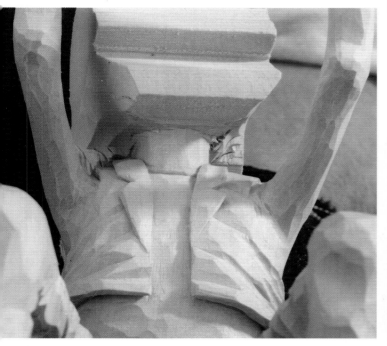

The hole that we drilled in the body to receive the neck was 3/4" in diameter; therefore, we want to make the neck 3/4" in diameter as well. We want this to be a very close fit. When you have followed all of the procedures for carving this neck you will understand why. This is the tight fit we want between the neck and the neck hole.

The second line, drawn below the reference line, corresponds to the thickness of the necklace.

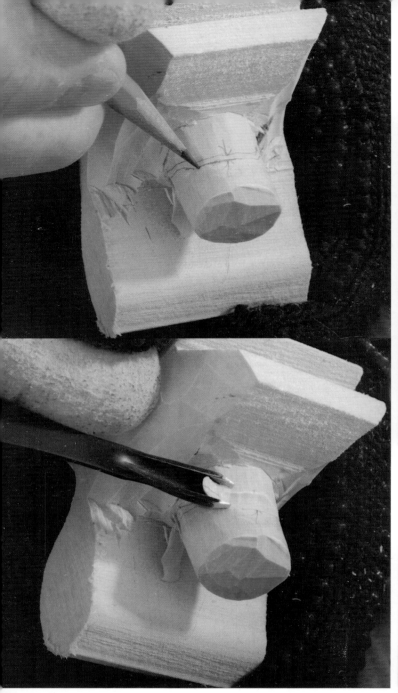

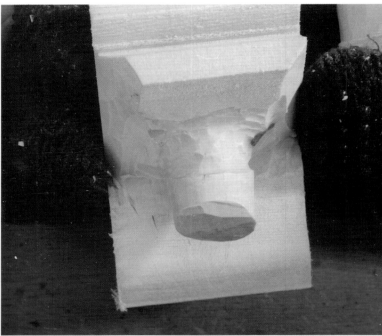

This is what the neck will look like once it is relieved.

Use a 1/4" deep gouge and round the neck down from the chin to this bottom line.

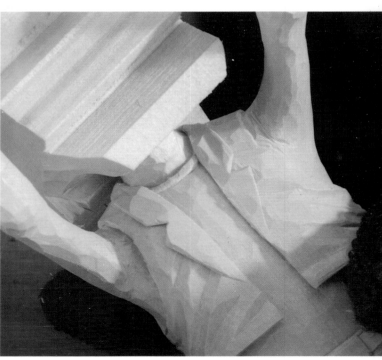

This is what the neck looks like inserted into the body. This neck carving technique makes the neck look as though it is actually part of the body extended under the necklace or whatever is used to hide the neck hole line.

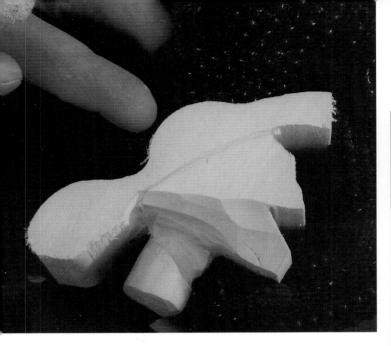

Connect the front and the back of the hair with an arched pencil line.

Divide the top of the head into two equal parts.

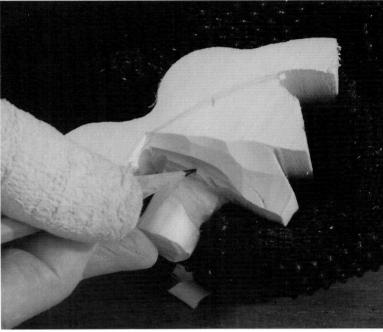

Divide the neck into two equal parts as well.

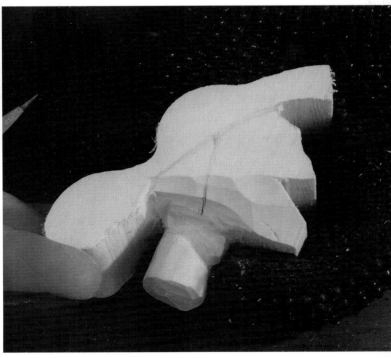

Connect the two dividing marks with a straight line. This line will become the front of the ear.

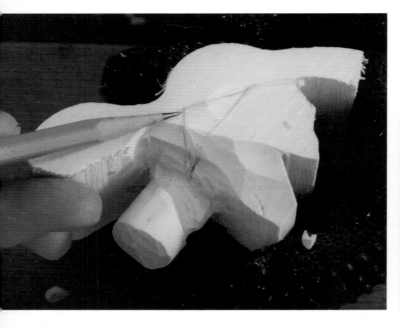

The back of the ear will fall along the line drawn here.

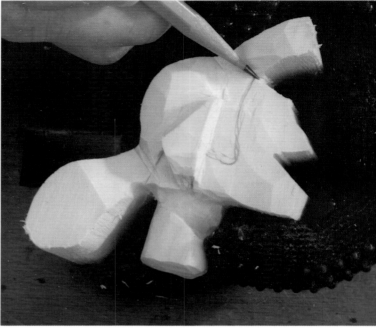

Draw in the sideburns.

Relieve the head, leaving the ear mound protruding from the side of the head, about like this.

Cut the sideburns in with a medium sized V tool.

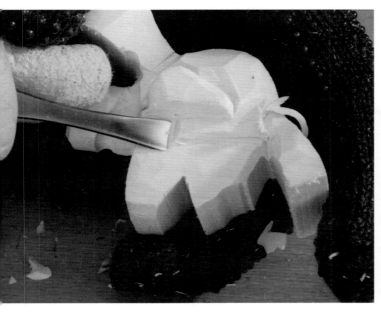

Relieve the side of the face to the bottom of the V cut.

Remove the front of the ear at a 45 degree angle to the depth of the sideburn.

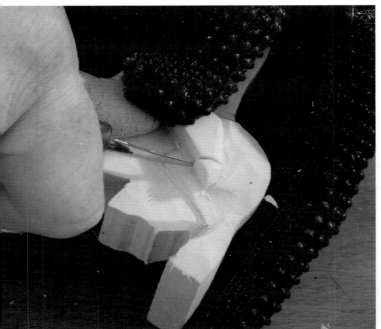

Cut the top of the ear in. Remove this triangle.

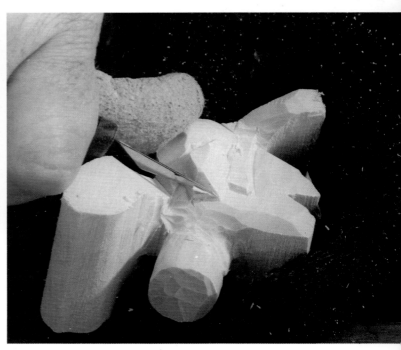

Clip off the bottom of the ear.

Cup the ear like so.

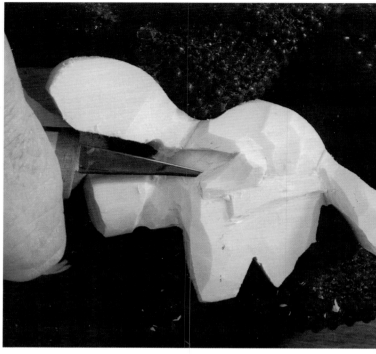

Remove the scored excess wood from behind the ear.

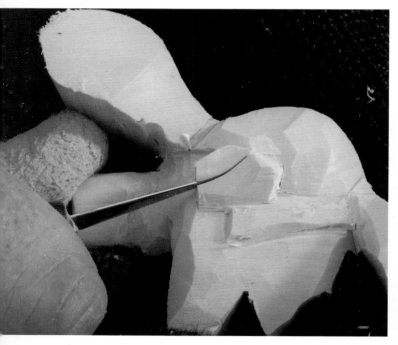

Score along the back of the ear, like this.

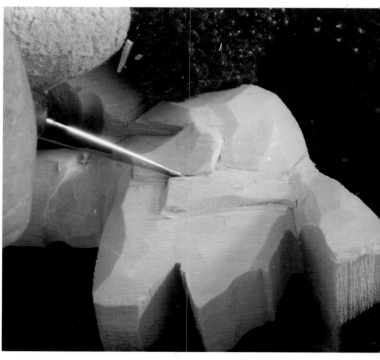

Score along the front of the ear between the sideburn and the ear.

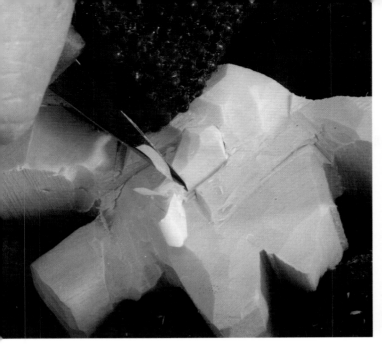

Undercut the sideburn so the ear appears to be part of the side of the face rather than a part of the sideburn.

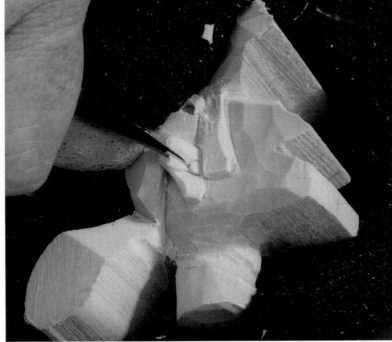

Using your knife, relieve the wood behind this tragus.

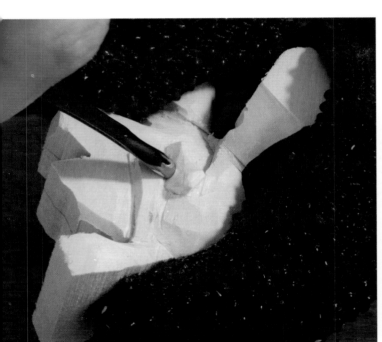

Take a 1/8" deep gouge and, at the angle shown, score the tragus into the ear.

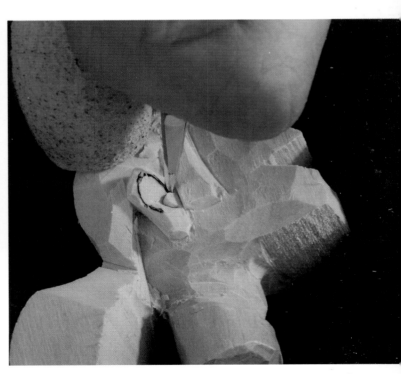

Score along the outside perimeter of the ear from the top of the tragus to a point in line with the bottom of the tragus.

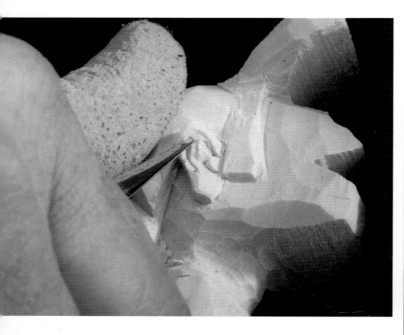

Relieve the ear below this scored line.

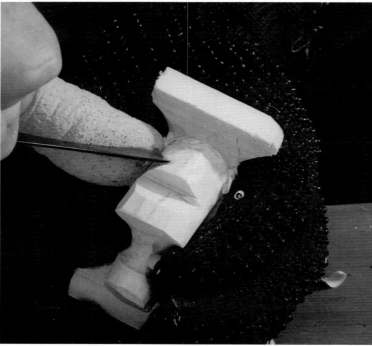

Round off the front of the head, better known as the face, from the front of the sideburns to the centerline.

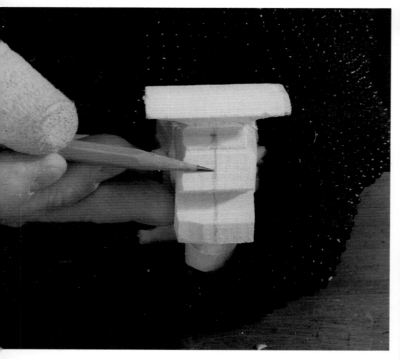

Draw a centerline on the face.

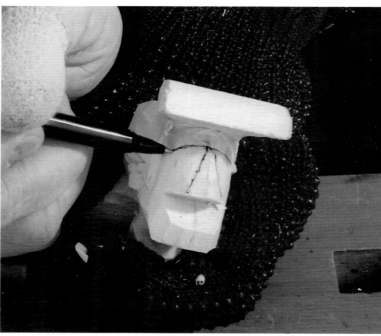

Sketch in the eyebrow line and each side of the nose.

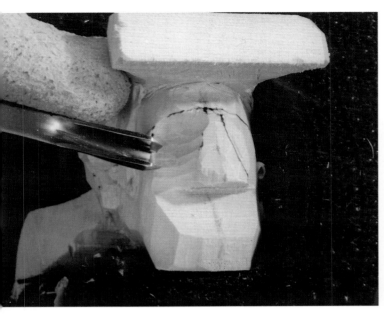

Using a 1/4" deep gouge, cut straight across the face, removing the wood between the eyebrow and the side of the nose.

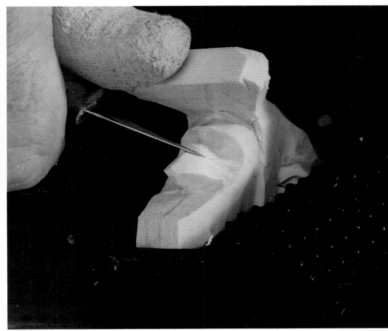

Round off the nose.

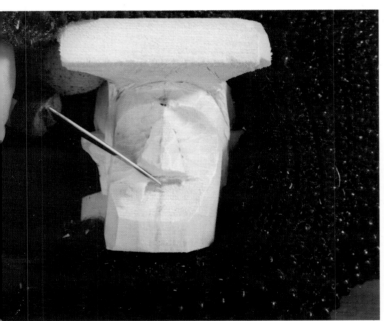

Clip the bottom of the nose at roughly this angle.

Round off both the mouth area underneath the nose and the side of the eye sockets.

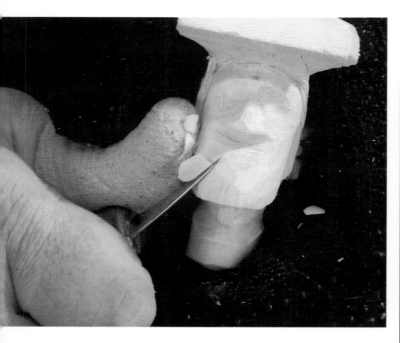

Shape the chin.

Cut these smile lines in with a medium sized V tool, carrying the cut up the side of the nose.

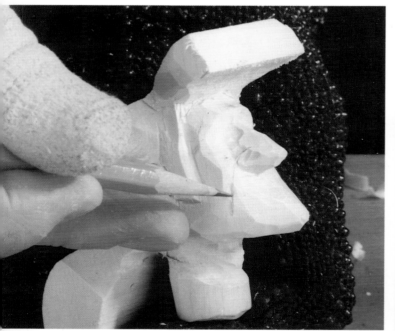

Draw smile lines as shown.

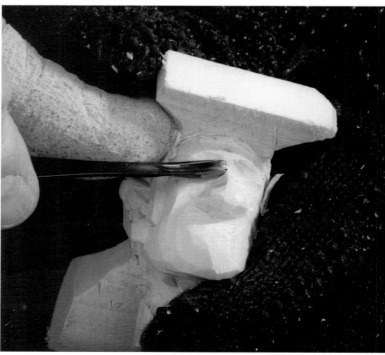

Relieve the upper portion of the nose above the smile line with the small gouge.

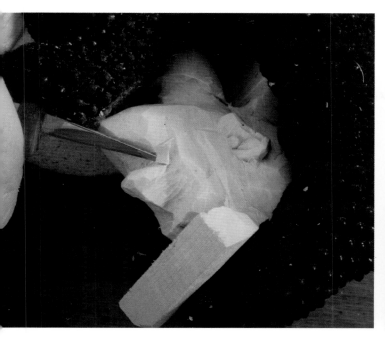

Relieve the mouth area under the nose to the bottom of the smile line V cut.

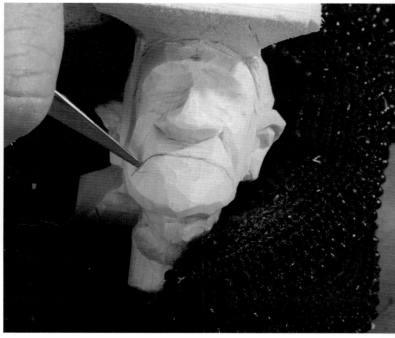

Score along this mouth line with the knife tip.

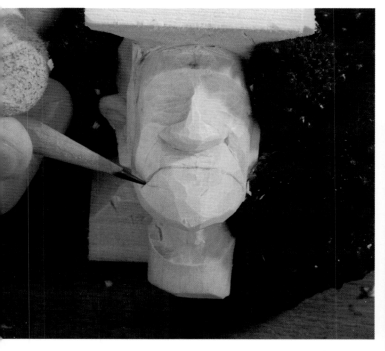

Draw the mouth in.

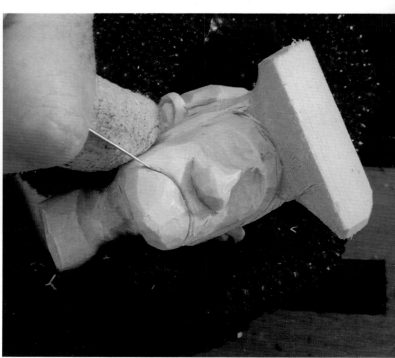

Using the knife tip, remove the top of the bottom lip at a 45 degree angle.

Remove the bottom of the top lip at a 45 degree angle as shown.

Remove a small chip from the corner of the mouth.

With the small 1/8" gouge, starting at the chip at the corner of the mouth, remove wood from below the lip to the thickness of the lower lip desired.

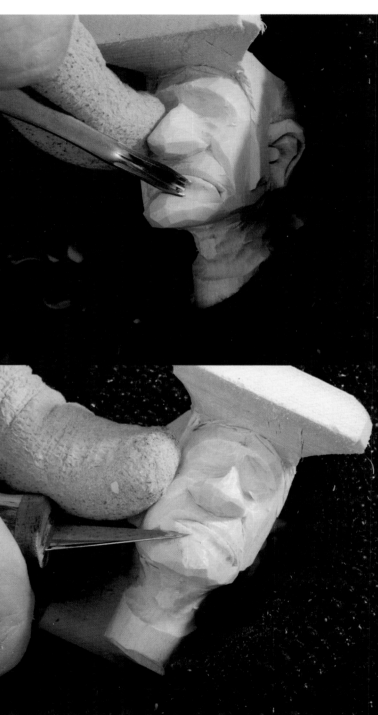

Relieving wood from the lower lip to the outer chin.

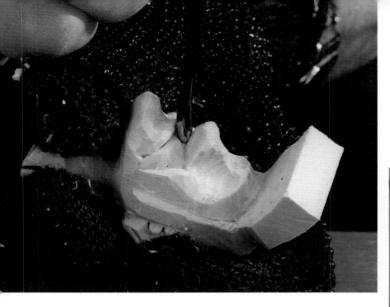

Continuing with the small 1/8" gouge, cut in the philtrum (the center channel running from the base of the nose to the upper lip) from the top of the upper lip to the bottom of the nose.

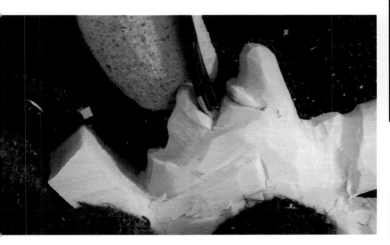

Using the same gouge, cut the nostrils in on both sides of the septum.

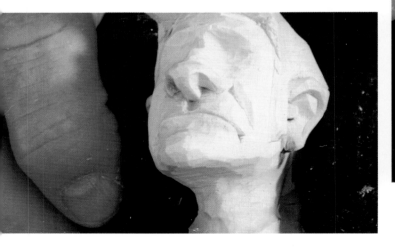

The philtrum and nostrils in place.

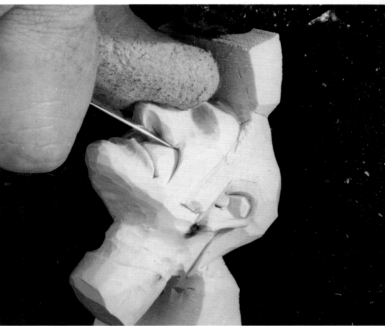

We have accented the smile line by undercutting it.

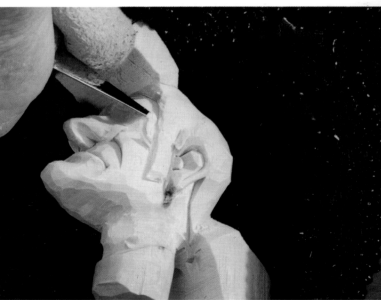

Use the knife to deepen the temples on either side of the head.

Sketch in the eyeballs. Try to make these symmetrical.

Relieve the eyeball from about the middle of the eyeball to the lower lid.

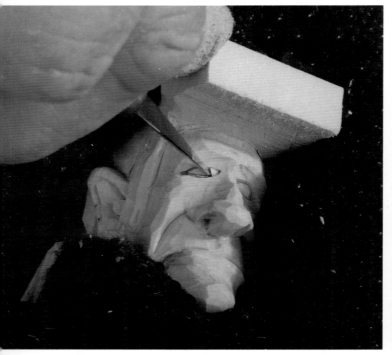

With your knife tip, clip out the inside and outside corners of the eyeball. Note the angle of the knife blade.

Relieve the upper part of the eyeball from about the center to the upper lid.

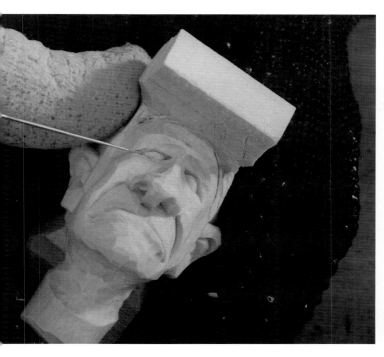

The rounded eyeballs.

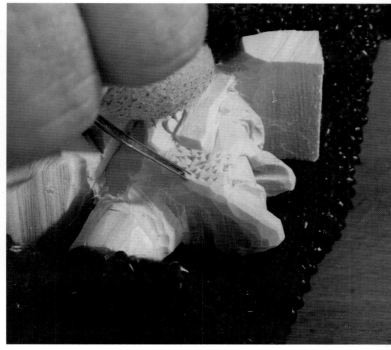

With a small V tool, carefully prick a three day beard shadow onto the face.

With your small V tool, carve in the upper eye lid.

Shape the front of the hair and ...

bring the back of the hair into a pony tail.

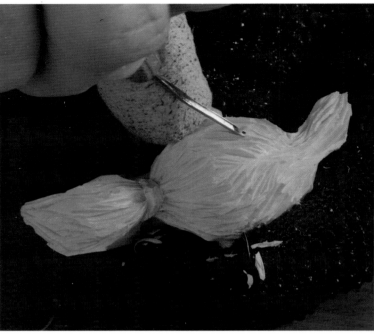

Now use a small V tool and carve in the irregular cuts of the hair as shown.

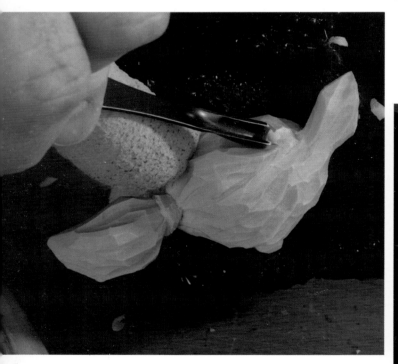

To begin the texturing of the hair, let's soften up this mound of wood on which we'll carve the hair by using a 1/4" deep gouge to set some fairly deep grooves into the wood.

With a small, deep gouge, separate the eyebrow mound between the eyes.

46

With your small V tool, cut some hair onto the eyebrow mounds.

Like so.

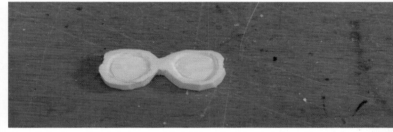

I decided to put some sunglasses on this old boy. We'll begin by carving the glass and frames.

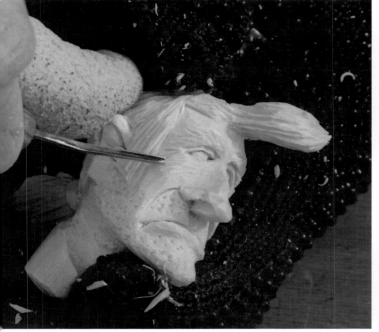

Use your small V tool to carve in some smile lines, age lines, and crows feet ... under the eyes, beside the eye, and along the forehead.

Attach the temple pieces to the glass and frame. That's all there is to that!

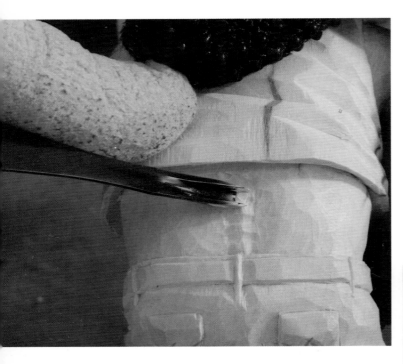

One final detail on this carving will be the backbone. Start by going across the backbone area, using a small, deep gouge. Go across about every 1/8", attempting to separate the vertebrae.

Finally, relieve the back itself, using a shallow gouge.

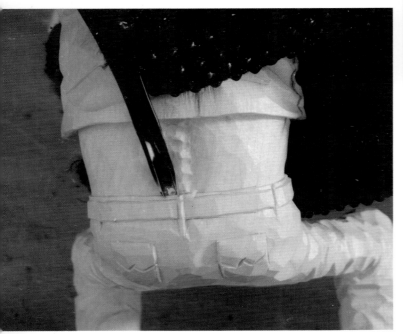

Then we will go from the bottom of the vest to the top of the pants on either side of the vertebrae to raise the spine.

Painting the Figure and Motorcycle

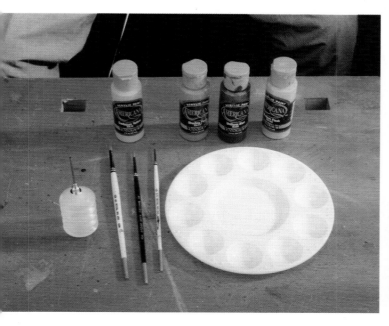

We're going to use Americana Acrylic Paints by Deco Art in a variety of colors which will be named as they are used. The brushes we'll use will vary in size from 00000 to a #5. I will use a plastic bubble palette and a glue dispenser for transferring water for the acrylic paint and water mixture.

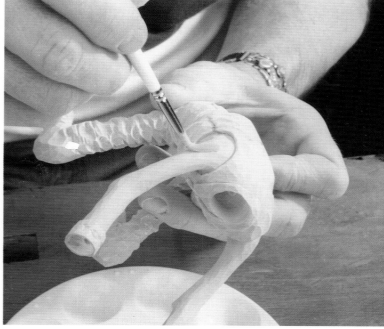

I'm using DA102 Medium Flesh to paint the fleshy surfaces of the body.

Most of the washes I use will start with this amount of paint in the bubble palette. I will fill that bubble with water and mix the paint and water together using the brush.

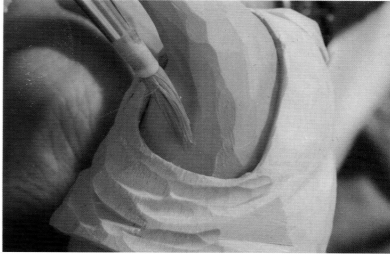

Use DA137 Shading Flesh to darken the values of this flesh tone around the arm holes of the vest, around the black leather bracelets on his wrists, and along the underside of the vest around his waist, and the around lower part of his torso at the pant line. This shading technique is called wet-on-wet, which means that the darker tone should be applied over the wet lighter tone. The paints diffuse, running into each other, and meld.

Let's use the darker Shading Flesh around the eyes, the nostrils, along each smile line, in the philtrum, beneath the lower lip, around the perimeter of the face along the hair line, behind the tragus in the ear, and along the outside perimeter of the ear.

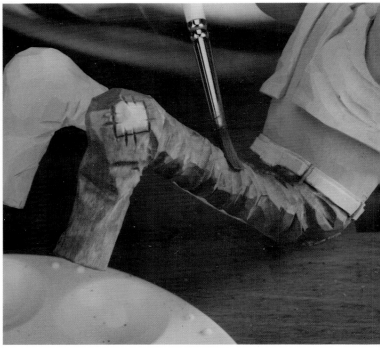

For the jeans, I'm using DA86, Uniform Blue.

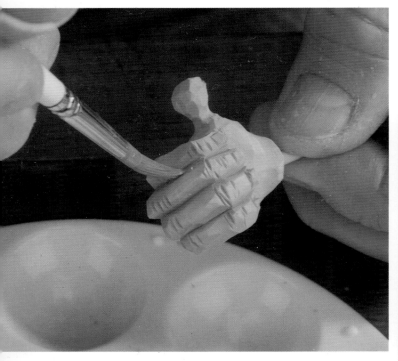

We'll also use the Shading Flesh along the finger separations, around the wrists, and on the finger nails.

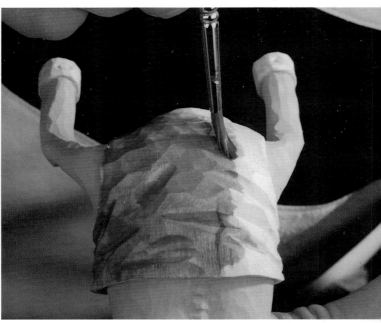

Deco Art makes several beautiful shades of purple; however, to prove that you can mix these pre-mixed acrylic colors I have decided to make my own purple from two parts of DA20 Calico Red and one part DA39 Victorian Blue. Apply this color to the vest.

I'm using this Soft Black wash and a technique called dry brushing to paint the stubble of beard. The dry brushing technique is one in which you load your brush with paint and, brushing across an absorbent paper, attempt to dry the brush, leaving some small amount of this paint in the nearly dry brush fibers. Then use the brush to apply what is left onto the surface to be painted.

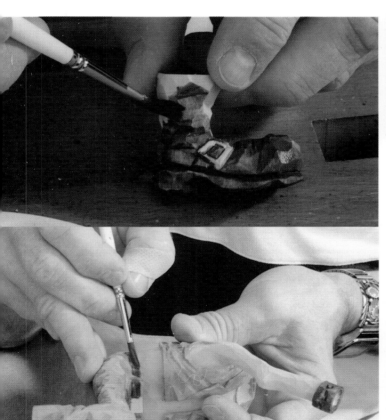

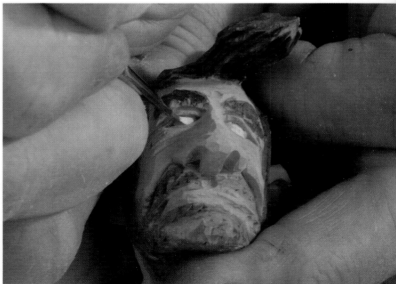

One of the great colors that Deco Art makes is DA155 Soft Black which is not as harsh as the Lamp Black produced by Deco Art and other companies. We'll use this Soft Black on the boots, the wrist bracelets, and belt.

Another of the great shades that Deco Art makes is DA164 Light Buttermilk. This shade of white is perfect for painting the eyeballs. I use it straight from the tube, without mixing this paint with water.

I'm using DA105 Blue-Grey Mist straight from the tube to paint the iris.

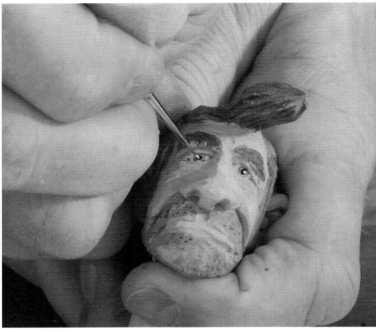

Use DA1 Titanium White to indicate reflected light on the eyeballs. This spot of white should appear in the same place in each eye.

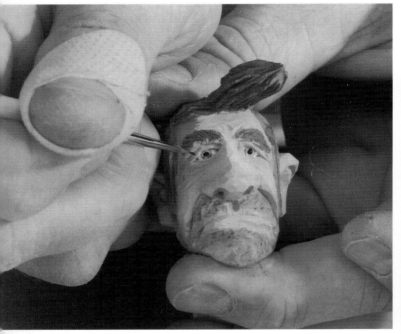

Use the Soft Black, undiluted, to paint the pupils. Keep those pupils and irises centered!

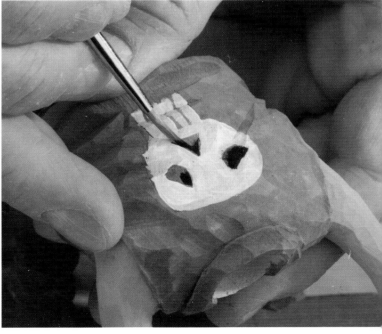

I'm using Titanium White to paint a skull on the back of the vest. Use Soft Black to darken in the eye sockets and nose opening.

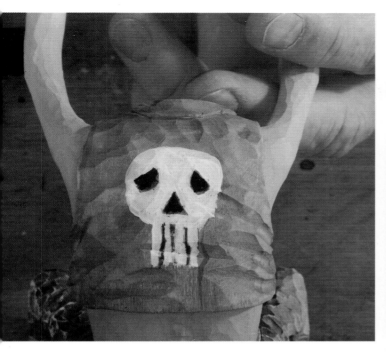

The finished skull.

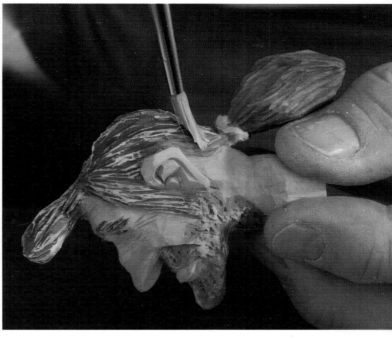

and to the hair.

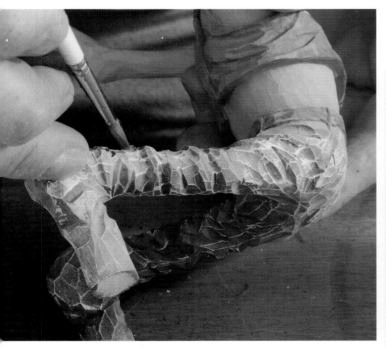

Use Titanium White and the dry brush technique to add some age to the jeans...

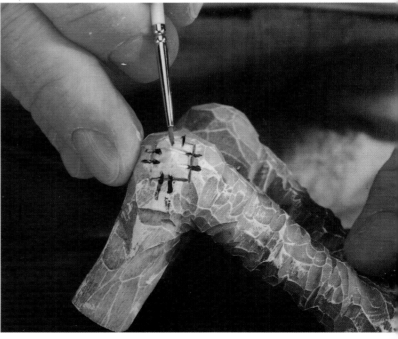

I use a mixture of Titanium White and Blue-Grey Mist to paint the patch and then Soft Black for the stitching.

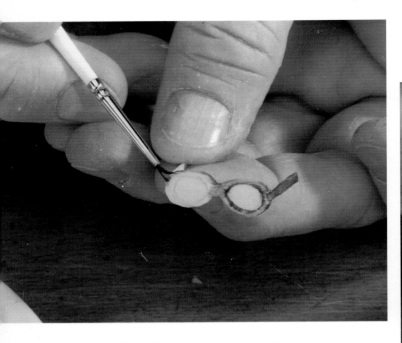

I'm using the Soft Black wash to paint the frames of the glasses.

the band holding the dude's pony tail...

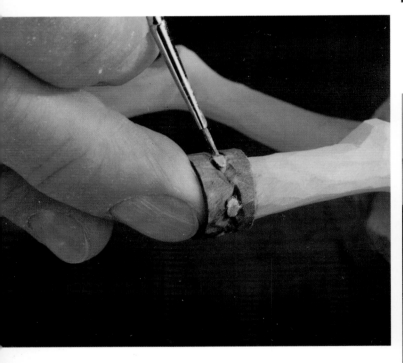

Use Deco Art Shimmering Silver to paint the metallic studs on the leather bracelets, the belt buckle, necklace...

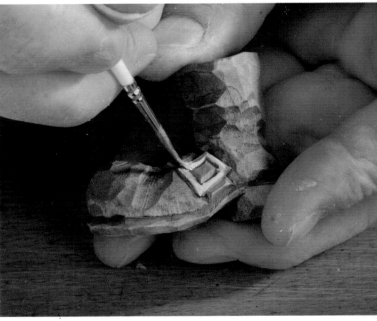

the buckles on the boots...

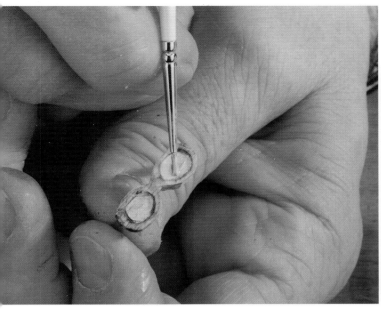

AND the lenses of the glasses.

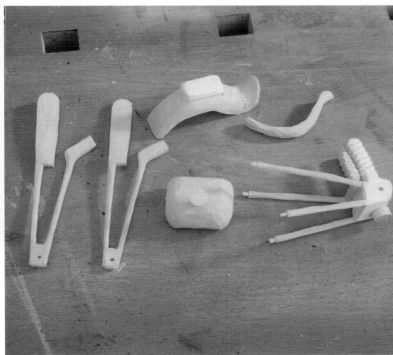

Use DA10 Cadmium Yellow to paint the side supports, the front forks, the gas tank, and the front and rear fenders.

I'm using a short bristled brush to apply an orange-red chalk on the tip of the nose, the cheeks, and the lips. I have tried using red washes for this effect, but I really like what the chalk does.

Use Soft Black to paint the engine, seat, tires, handle grips, and the small pack on the back of the rear fender.

Use undiluted Silver and the dry brush technique to highlight the cooling fins on the cylinders.

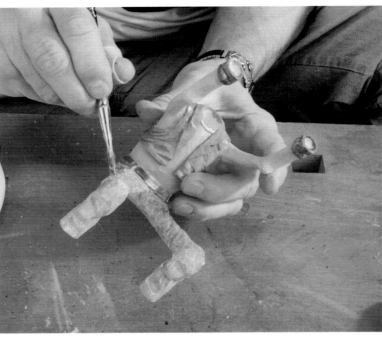

Use DS14 Deco Art Matte Varnish to seal each piece of this carving—that includes the motorcycle rider and the motorcycle.

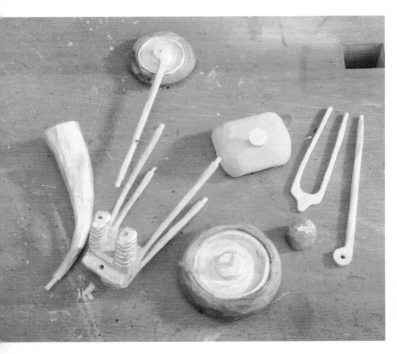

Dilute the Shimmering Silver, by about 50% with water, and paint the items shown with this wash.

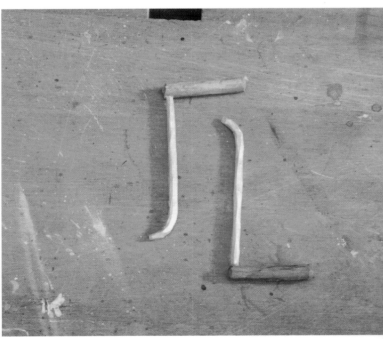

And finally, paint the handlebar assemblies Shimmering Silver.

Once all of your pieces have been sealed with the Matte Varnish and have been allowed to dry, apply a liberal coat of antiquing mixture to all the pieces. This antiquing mixture consists of four parts Watco Satin Finish Clear Wax and one part Watco Satin Finish Dark Wax. The darkness of this mixture can be varied by adding more clear or dark wax to this basic mixture.

Allow the wax antiquing solution to dry and then—using a soft horsehair shoe brush or equivalent power driven brush—buff all the carved pieces until a soft shine is produced. Buff very carefully around some of your thinner pieces.

Insert the head into the body and the hands into the arms. It will not be necessary to glue either of these in place.

Let's begin our assembly by gluing the glasses in place with Super Glue Gel.

Use a 1/8" dowel to connect the two side supports and the rear wheel together. Use glue to attach the front struts to the side supports.

Insert the sissy bar into the rear fender. Glue the rear fender to the rear wheel and the seat to the side supports.

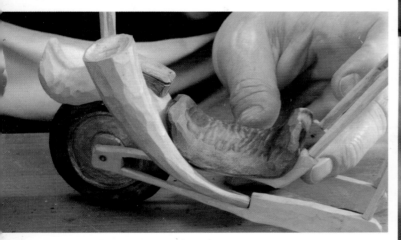

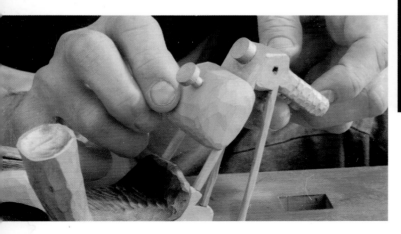

Glue the gas tank in place.

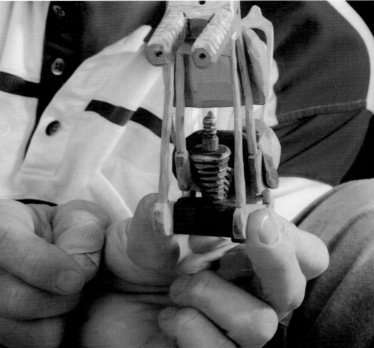

Glue the motor in place.

The front wheel, front supports, and front fender are assembled and glued in place.

The front assembly and the rear of the bike are now together.

Place the motorcycle rider on the seat of the bike, inserting his legs into the boots, and inserting the handlebar assemblies into both the hands and the front struts. Glue these items in place. Add the headlight to complete the bike. Mount the motorcycle on a base of your choice, using 1/8" dowels extended into both the base and the bottom of the wheels.

Gallery

(carved biker)

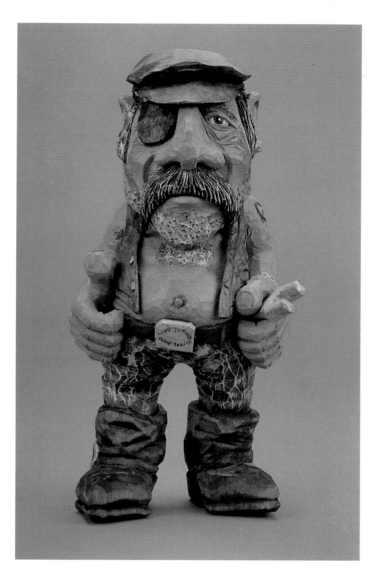

Carved from Steve Prescott's Blockhead Roughout.

Carved from a Roughout that can be ordered from Larry Yudis at the Woodcraft Shop, 2724 State St., Bettendorf, Iowa 52722.

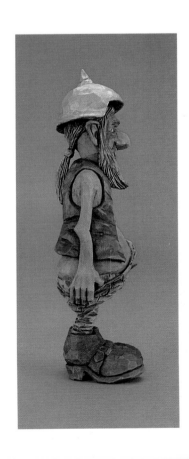

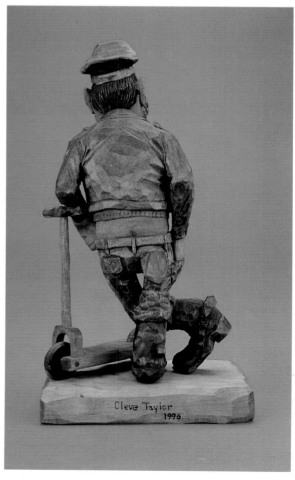

Cleve Taylor
1996

This carving was done by Will Hayden from Vancouver, Washington.

Above:
This carving was completed by Donna Healy from Caldwell, Idaho.

This carving was done by Virgil Butler from Boise, Idaho.

This carving was completed by Donna's husband, Ivan "Ike" Healy.